CAROLYN KANJURO is a writer and creative collaborator.
She has taught meditation, theater, and contemplative archery
to children throughout North America.

NAN LAWSON is an illustrator who has worked on a wide variety of
books from YA book covers to lift-the-flap board books. She's also a
regular contributor to several art galleries across the country. During her
free time she loves to read books while sipping coffee and looking out at
the mountains from her cozy living room. Nan lives in Los Angeles with
her husband, two-year-old daughter, and two lazy cats.

Bala Kids
An imprint of Shambhala Publications, Inc.
4720 Walnut Street
Boulder, Colorado 80301
www.shambhala.com

9 8 7 6 5 4 3 2 1

First Edition
Printed in China

⊗ This edition is printed on acid-free paper that meets the
American National Standards Institute Z39.48 Standard.
♲ Shambhala makes every effort to print on recycled paper.
For more information please visit www.shambhala.com.

Bala Kids is distributed worldwide by Penguin Random House, Inc., and its subsidiaries.

Designed by Kara Plikaitis

Library of Congress Cataloging-in-Publication Data
Names: Kanjuro, Carolyn, author.
Title: Sit with me: meditation for kids in seven easy steps / written by Carolyn Kanjuro;
illustrations by Nan Lawson.
Description: Boulder, Colorado: Bala Kids, 2020. | Audience: Ages 3-8. | Audience: Grades K-1. |
Summary: "You can squat like a frog or lounge like a cat–but if you want to sit like a
buddha easy and free, there are seven key steps for taking your seat. Sit with Me invites kids
of all ages to learn meditation through lyrical verse and playful illustrations, showing how
everyone is capable of sitting still, taking a breath, and letting their mind rest. The book includes
step-by-step instructions to show kids the correct posture and state of mind to best utilize
meditation in their daily lives."—Provided by publisher.
Identifiers: LCCN 2019040811 | ISBN 9781611807479 (hardback)
Subjects: LCSH: Meditation—Buddhism—Juvenile literature.
Classification: LCC: BQ5612 .K36118 2020 | DDC 294.3/4435083—dc23
LC record available at https://lccn.loc.gov/2019040811

SIT
WITH ME

MEDITATION for KIDS in SEVEN EASY STEPS

CAROLYN KANJURO   ILLUSTRATED by NAN LAWSON

bala kids

You can sit like a duck

or lounge like a cat

or squat like a frog

or hang like a bat.

You can chill like a moose,

hunker down like a bear,

perch like an owl,

or flop like a hare.

But if you want to sit like a buddha,
easy and free,
just like the Buddha
under the old Bodhi tree,

there are seven key points
from your head to your feet
to position yourself
for taking your seat.

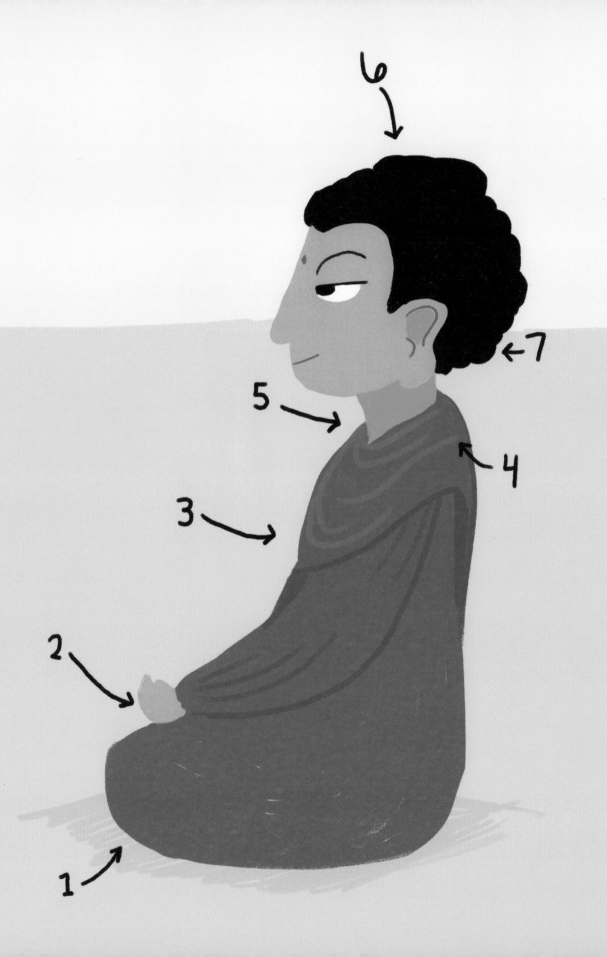

First, sit down
in one spot
like a singular dot.

It's strangely profound
when you sit yourself down,
cross your legs,
and relax your knees to the ground.

Next, place your hands
on your thighs or your knees
to take up the posture
we call "royal ease."

Without fidgeting or squirming,
keep your palms facing down
as you sit still
with your butt on the ground
like a queen or king,
just lounging around.

Third, keep your spine
straight like an arrow
or coins stacked on a plate.
But don't clench your muscles
or grow stiff like a board:
if you tighten too much,
you're sure to get sore.

Instead, imagine a string
at the top of your head
gently pulling you upward
with effortless ease
to keep your spine straight
for as long as you please.

Fourth, keep your chest open,
your shoulders apart.
Don't crumple forward
and close up your heart.

Like the wings of a vulture,
balanced and wide,
open yourself
with nothing to hide.

Fifth, keep your chin
just a little tucked in
to make a straight line
with your head and your spine.

If you raise up your head,
you'll start thinking like mad,
and a head hanging low
makes you sleepy or sad.

So, sit with your chin
just a little tucked in,
and notice the balance
it brings you within.

Sixth, keep your eyes open.
Gaze softly, with ease.
There's no need to grasp
anything that you see.

Just let your eyes rest
about three or four feet
down on the ground
in front of your seat.

And last, with your mouth
slightly open,
relaxing your chin,
place your tongue on the roof
so no bugs can fly in.

Alright, let's have one quick review:

4 Shoulders in balance and open, a great vulture's wings

3 Back straight as an arrow, pulled up by a string

2 Hands on your thighs with your palms facing down

1 Butt down, legs crossed, knees relaxed to the ground

As you breathe,
let your thoughts come and go
like the rain or a fog
or a fine, feathery snow.

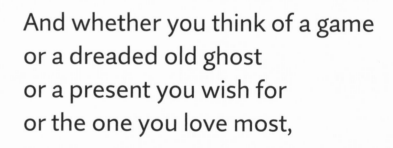

And whether you think of a game
or a dreaded old ghost
or a present you wish for
or the one you love most,

there's no need to pull them
or push them away,
or chase them or punch them
or ask them to stay.

Simply let everything be
as you sit like a buddha,
easy and free,
just like the Buddha
under the great Bodhi tree.

Hi there! I'm Justa Bug.
Traveling on the Buddha's road
I've picked up a thing or two—
like this seven-point posture,
which will perfectly do
for a bug like me or a kid like you,
if you want to be a buddha, too.

DATE DUE